AUTHOR'S BIO

My daughter and I created this book to help children with their fear. It was inspired by Leigh developing a fear of her kindergarten's teacher. We wanted to illustrate how we got through this emotion.

DESCRIPTION

This book is to help children understand the emotion of fear. Where it comes from and insight on how to over come it. Through the interaction between a daughter and father. It provides great insight for young developing minds. While being a fun read!!!

It was early winter, and snow lined the streets of Happyton.
In a huuuugggggeeee green house up the hill, filled with bright lights, an alarm clock was blaring, beep, beep, beep.

- Wake up, wake up, princess. It is time for school. Lai's father said.

-Lai replied: Dad, can I stay home from school today?
-Huh, why? Are you sick?
-Lai shook her head no.

-Why then, princess?
-It is Ms. Red. She is soooooo mean and she scares me.
Ms. Red is Lai's kindergarten teacher.

-She is reeaaalllllyyyy tall, with stinky breath.

-She is reeaaalllllyyyy loud, with frizzy hair.

-She is reeaaalllllyyyy wide, with jagged teeth.

-And alllwaaayys yells at the class.

-I understand. Lai's father replied.

-As he consoled Lai, he said to her: Let's make breakfast.

As the pancakes and bacon cooked, he turned to her.
-He said: Lai, I wish we could like everyone, but some people are in our lives only for reasons or seasons.
-Sometimes, being unaware in situations can lead to fear.

-Princess, Ms. Red is here to educate and help prepare you for the world, baby girl.
-She has reeaaallllyyyy stinky breath, but it helps you focus on school.
Breakfast is served. Lai takes a bite of her breakfast, and Ms. Red gets a liiitttttlllleee smaller in her mind.

-Sometimes with more information, your view becomes clearer.

-She has reeaaalllllyyyy frizzy hair because she is shocked at how smart the class is.

-She's reeaaalllllyyyy loud, so everyone can hear the lesson.

Lai takes a bite, and Ms. Red gets a liiitttttlllleee smaller in her mind.
-She has reeaaalllllyyyy jagged teeth, so she can eat apples better.
-She is reeaaalllllyyyy tall because you are reeaaalllllyyyy small.

Lai takes a bite, and Ms. Red gets a liiittttttllleee smaller in her mind.
-She seems reeaaalllllyyyy wide because you are reeaaalllllyyyy skinny.

-See, Lai, being unaware can lead to fear, and with a liiittttlllleee more information, your vision can become clearer.
Lai took her last bite, and Ms. Red disappeared from her mind.

Then Ms. Red reappeared in her mind.
She looked cheerful and happy.
-Lai spoke: Dad, let's go to school.
I am ready!

The End!